LIFE'S LITTLE
TREASURE BOOK

On
Hope

H. JACKSON BROWN, JR.

RUTLEDGE HILL PRESS®
NASHVILLE, TENNESSEE
A Thomas Nelson Company

Published by Rutledge Hill Press, a Thomas Nelson Company, Nashville, Tennessee 37214.

Typography by D&T/Bailey Typesetting, Inc., Nashville, Tennessee

Illustrations by Ken Morris

Jacket Illustration by Greg King

Book design by Harriette Bateman

ISBN: 1-55853-419-9

Printed in the Republic of China

3 4 5 6 7 8 9—03 02 01 00

INTRODUCTION

*H*ope is a rare and precious gift, easily given and always welcomed. Whether we're "hoping for the best" or encouraging a friend to "never lose hope," we recognize the power of hope to create and sustain a successful and joyful life. Regardless of our circumstances, our spirits are always lifted and encouraged by the realization that something different, better, or more challenging lies right around the bend.

Hope is the magic carpet that transports us from the present moment into the realm of infinite possibilities. Physicians acknowledge the power of hope to heal. It is hope that sends soldiers off to war and hope that brings the hearts and future of two strangers together for what becomes a lifetime commitment. Was there ever a lover who didn't live on hope? "I hope she loves me." "I hope she loves me as much as I love her." "I hope we will love each other forever."

Benjamin Franklin wrote that he who lives upon hope will die fasting.

That's true to the degree that we hope and do little else. Hope is not a resting place but a starting point—a cactus, not a cushion. Like my dad used to say, "Work and hope, but don't hope more than you work."

We all agree that hope is an indispensable and inevitable feature of the human spirit. Alexander Pope observed, "Hope springs eternal in the human breast." Perhaps that is what makes the human condition so unique and ultimately so promising. For while we may lose heart, we never have to lose hope.

Twix the optimist and pessimist
The difference is droll;
The optimist sees the doughnut
But the pessimist sees the hole.

—McLandburg Wilson

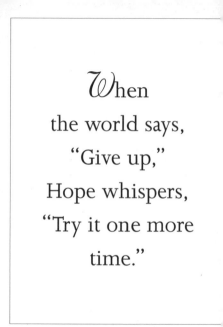

When
the world says,
"Give up,"
Hope whispers,
"Try it one more
time."

$\mathcal{I}$'ve learned that ...

. . . I don't feel my age as long as I focus on my dreams instead of my regrets. —Age 83

. . . you shouldn't go through life with a catcher's mitt on both hands. You need to be able to throw something back.

—Age 64

On the darkest night the stars
shine most brightly.

∾

I am not afraid of tomorrow for
I have seen yesterday and I
love today.

—William White

$\mathcal{N}$ever deprive
someone of hope;
it may be all
they have.

*It takes courage to live—
courage and strength and hope
and humor. And courage and
strength and hope and humor
have to be bought and paid for
with pain and work and
progress and tears.*

—Jerome P. Fleishman

Success is not
tomorrow;
Success is today.
Do it now! Get it done!
Success is on the way.

—Unknown

*R*emember that life's most
treasured moments often
come unannounced.

☙

*H*ope would as soon dine
with a pauper as a prince.

Just as despair can come to one only from other human beings, hope, too, can be given to one only by other human beings.

—Elie Wiesel

❧

Never give up on what you really want to do. The person with big dreams is more powerful than one with all the facts.

$\mathcal{I}$'ve learned that . . .

. . . being a grandparent is God's compensation for growing older. —Age 64

. . . life's greatest joys usually show up unexpectedly and often in the most uncommon places. —Age 27

You are as old as your doubt, your fear, your despair. The way to keep young is to keep your faith young. Keep your self-confidence young. Keep your hope young.

—Dr. L. F. Phelan

*W*hen facing a difficult task, act as though it is impossible to fail. If you are going after Moby Dick, take along the tartar sauce.

*P*rotect your enthusiasm
from the negativity of others.

∾

Strong hope is a much greater
stimulant of life than any single
realized joy could be.

—Friedrich Nietzsche

We are all in the gutter, but some of us are looking at the stars.

—Oscar Wilde

∾

Everything that is done in the world is done by hope.

—Martin Luther

$\mathscr{I}$'ve learned that . . .

. . . physical strength is measured by what we can carry; spiritual strength by what we can bear.   —Age 49

. . . life is worth living when you are giving others moments of happiness and hope.   —Age 82

$\mathcal{N}$ever give up on anybody.
Miracles happen every day.

❧

$\mathcal{L}$eave everything a little
better than you found it.

❧

$\mathcal{L}$earn to listen. Opportunity
sometimes knocks very softly.

*W*ork and hope, but don't hope more than you work.

To travel hopefully is better
than to arrive.

—Sir James Jeans

❧

The charm of fishing is that it
is the pursuit of what is elusive
but obtainable, a perpetual
series of occasions for hope.

—John Buchan

$\mathcal{N}$ine Requisites for Contented Living

1. Health enough to make work a pleasure.
2. Wealth enough to support your needs.
3. Strength enough to battle with difficulties and overcome them.
4. Grace enough to confess your sins and forsake them.

5. Patience enough to toil until some good is accomplished.
6. Charity enough to see some good in your neighbor.
7. Love enough to move you to be useful and helpful to others.
8. Faith enough to make real the things of God.
9. Hope enough to remove all anxious fears concerning the future.

—Goethe

Lay hold of the hope set before us. This hope we have as an anchor of the soul, both sure and steadfast.

—Hebrews 6:18–19

❧

Make it a habit to do nice things for people who'll never find out.

$\mathscr{I}$'ve learned that . . .

. . . angels really do exist on earth. —Age 43

. . . people tend to rise to accomplishments they thought were beyond them if you show them by your confidence that they can do it. —Age 53

∾

Ah, Hope! What would life be, stripped of thy encouraging smiles, that teach us to look behind the dark clouds of to-day, for the golden beams that are to gild the morrow.

—Susanna Moodie

Swing for the fence.

❧

At the end of your days, be leaning forward—not falling backward.

❧

Spend your life lifting people up, not putting people down.

With every rising of the sun
Think of your life as just begun.
The past has shriveled and buried deep
All yesterdays; there let them sleep.
Concern yourself with but today,
Woo it, and teach it to obey
Your will and wish. Since time began
Today has been the friend of man.

—Ella Wheeler Wilcox

$\mathcal{P}$ray. There is immeasurable
power in it.

❧

$\mathcal{C}$all a nursing home or
retirement center and ask for
a list of the residents who
seldom get mail or visitors.
Send them a card several
times a year. Sign it,
"Someone who thinks you
are very special."

The natural flights of the human mind are not from pleasure to pleasure, but from hope to hope.

—Samuel Johnson

∿

If you have ever planted a seed, you know the power and promise of hope.

Some men see things as
they are and say, "Why?"
I dream of things that
never were and say,
"Why not?"

—George Bernard Shaw

$\mathcal{I}$'ve learned that . . .

. . . singing "Amazing Grace" can lift my spirits for hours. —Age 49

. . . no matter how bad it gets, when my child hugs my neck and kisses me and says, "Don't worry, everything will be OK," I know I'll be able to make it.

—Age 28

*R*emember the credo of Walt Disney: Think. Believe. Dream. Dare.

∾

*W*hen someone lets you down, don't give up on them.

Hope in every sphere of life is a privilege that attaches to action. No action, no hope.

—Peter Levi

∾

Hope dies unless you feed it.

—English proverb

$\mathcal{L}$ives of great men all remind us
We can make our lives sublime,
And, departing, leave behind us
Footprints on the sands of time;

Footprints, that perhaps another,
Sailing o'er life's solemn main,
A forlorn and shipwrecked brother,
Seeing, shall take heart again.

Let us then be up and doing,
With a heart for any fate;
Still achieving, still pursuing,
Learn to labor and to wait.

—Henry Wadsworth Longfellow

A hopeful heart never underestimates the power of love.

A hopeful heart never underestimates the power of forgiveness.

A hopeful heart never underestimates the power of a kind word or deed.

*K*eep a special notebook.
Every night before going to
bed, write down something
beautiful that you saw during
the day.

∿

*W*elcome the unexpected!
Opportunities rarely come in
neat, predictable packages.

We judge of man's wisdom by his hope.

—Ralph Waldo Emerson

*H*ope is to dreams what baking powder is to biscuits.

∾

*H*old puppies, kittens, and babies any time you get the chance.

$\mathcal{I}$'ve learned that . . .

. . . many people give up
just when they are about to
achieve success. —Age 48

. . . the secret of growing old
gracefully is never to lose your
enthusiasm for meeting new
people and seeing new places.
—Age 75

There is a medicine for despair—we call it hope.

࿇

I always prefer to believe the best of everybody—it saves so much trouble.

—Rudyard Kipling

Keep your face to the

sunshine and you cannot

see the shadows.

—Helen Keller

$\mathcal{N}$ever give up on a dream just because of the length of time it will take to accomplish it. The time will pass anyway.

∾

$\mathcal{B}$e joyful in hope, patient in affliction, faithful in prayer.

—Romans 12:12

$\mathscr{B}$e grateful for all you have,
even if it's not enough.

∾

$\mathscr{H}$ope is definitely not the same
thing as optimism. It is not the
conviction that something will
turn out well, but the certainty
that something makes sense,
regardless of how it turns out.

—Václav Havel

$\mathcal{I}$'ve learned that ...

. . . life is like a blind date.
Sometimes you just have to
have a little faith.   —Age 23

. . . what we have done for
ourselves alone dies with us.
What we have done for others
and the world remains and is
immortal.   —Age 89

Keep a couple of your favorite inspirational books by your bedside.

❧

Hope affects everything; let your hook always be cast. In the stream where you least expect it, there will be a fish.

—Ovid

*C*ommitment to a
big dream
always brings
reinforcements.

Of all the forces that make for a better world, none is so indispensable, none so powerful as hope. Without hope man is only half alive.

—Charles Sawyer

❦

One door never shuts but another one opens.

He who has health, has hope; and he who has hope, has everything.

—Arabian proverb

*W*ith every rising of the sun
Think of your life as just begun.

The past has cancelled and
buried deep
All yesterdays. There let them sleep.

Concern yourself with but today.
Guard it, and teach it to obey.

Your will and plan. Since time began
Today has been the friend of man.

You and today. A soul sublime
And the great heritage of time.

With God himself to bind the twain,
Go forth, brave heart! Attain! Attain!

—Ella Wheeler Wilcox

Life is no brief candle to me, it is a sort of splendid torch which I've got hold of for the moment and I want to make it burn as bright as possible before handing it on to a future generation.

—George Bernard Shaw

*H*ope abandons only those
who turn her away.

◌

*W*hen you are worried, give
your troubles to God; He will
be up all night anyway.

Do what you can, with what you have, wherever you are.

—Theodore Roosevelt

❧

Not all of us will have the opportunity to do great things well, but we all have the opportunity to do small things well.

Life affords no higher pleasures than that of surmounting difficulties, passing from one step of success to another, forming new wishes and seeing them gratified. He that labors in any great or laudable undertaking has his fatigues first supported by hope and aftermath rewarded by joy.

—Samuel Johnson

$\mathscr{I}$'ve learned that . . .

. . . for a happy day, look for something bright and beautiful in nature. Listen for a beautiful sound, speak a kind word to some person, and do something nice for someone without their knowledge.

—Age 85

*O*ur greatest
possession is hope.

The important things of life will not perish. The greatest things will endure—faith, hope, love, and the moral nature of man.

—Claude M. Fuess

∾

A hopeful person is someone who takes along a camera when he goes fishing.

$\mathcal{I}$ve learned that . . .

. . . you should never tell a child that his dreams are unlikely or outlandish. Few things are more humiliating, and what a tragedy it would be if he believed it.   —Age 18

. . . the greatest physician in the world is hope and optimism.   —Age 41

I steer my bark with hope
. . . leaving fear astern.
—Thomas Jefferson

Remember the tea kettle:
though up to its neck in hot
water, it continues to sing.
—Unknown

Life is often hard. You can let it grind you down or polish you up.

∾

We should not let our fears hold us back from pursuing our hopes.

—John F. Kennedy

$\mathscr{I}$ never expect to lose. Even when I'm the underdog, I still prepare a victory speech.

—HJB

❧

$\mathscr{I}$t's not over 'til it's over.

—Yogi Berra

Not knowing when

the dawn will come,

I open every door.

—Emily Dickinson

$\mathcal{I}$'ve learned that . . .

. . . a pat on the back and a sincere "You're doing a great job" can make someone's day.

—Age 49

. . . no matter how dreary, miserable, or bitter the weather, birds always can be heard singing.

—Age 52

The marvelous richness of human experience would lose something of rewarding joy if there was no limitations to overcome. The hilltop hour would not be half so wonderful if there were no dark valleys to traverse.

—Helen Keller

The great essentials
of happiness are:
something to do,
something to love,
and something to
hope for.

$\mathcal{M}$y message to you is:
Be courageous! Be as
brave as your fathers
before you. Have faith!
Go forward.

—Thomas A. Edison

Every problem has two handles. You can grab it by the handle of fear or the handle of hope.

❧

After all, tomorrow is another day.
—Margaret Mitchell

There is no medicine like hope,

no incentive so great,

and no tonic so powerful

as expectation of

something tomorrow.

—O. S. Mardan

I've learned that . . .

. . . the only thing harder than being a Christian is being a Chicago Cubs fan.

—Age 55

. . . a personal emotional crisis or illness is often a prelude to personal growth and transformation.   —Age 36

*H*ope is a cactus not a cushion. It should make you jump up and do something.

∾

Only those who will risk going too far can possibly find out how far one can go.

—T. S. Eliot

$\mathcal{B}$e bold and courageous.
When you look back on your
life, you will regret the things
you didn't do more than the
ones you did.

❧

$\mathcal{P}$roblems are like a box of
Crackerjack. If you look
closely enough, you will
always find a prize.

Keep away from people who try to belittle your ambitions. Small people always do that, but the really great make you feel that you, too, can become great.

—Mark Twain

*H*ope is putting faith to work when doubting would be easier.

∾

There is one thing which gives radiance to everything. It is the idea of something around the corner.

—G. K. Chesterton

$\mathcal{I}$ve learned that . . .

. . . it pays to believe in miracles. And to tell the truth, I've seen several. —Age 73

. . . every day you should reach out and touch someone. People love that human touch—holding hands, a warm hug, or just a friendly pat on the back.

—Age 85

When a friend or loved one
becomes ill, remember that
hope and positive thinking
are strong medicines.

∽

Every so often let your spirit
of adventure triumph over
your good sense.

While admiring your neighbor's lawn across the fence, don't miss the roses blooming at your feet.

❧

What lies behind us and what lies before us are tiny matters compared to what lies within us.

—Ralph Waldo Emerson

An expert at anything was once a beginner.

∾

Cherish your dreams, hold tight to your ideals, march boldly to the music that only you can hear. Great lives are built by moving forward, never by looking back.

Deep within man dwell those slumbering powers; powers that would astonish him, that he never dreamed of possessing; forces that would revolutionize his life if aroused and put into action.

—Orison Swett Marden

Nothing will ever be attempted if all possible objections must first be overcome.

—Samuel Johnson

❧

Remember that half the joy of achievement is in the anticipation.

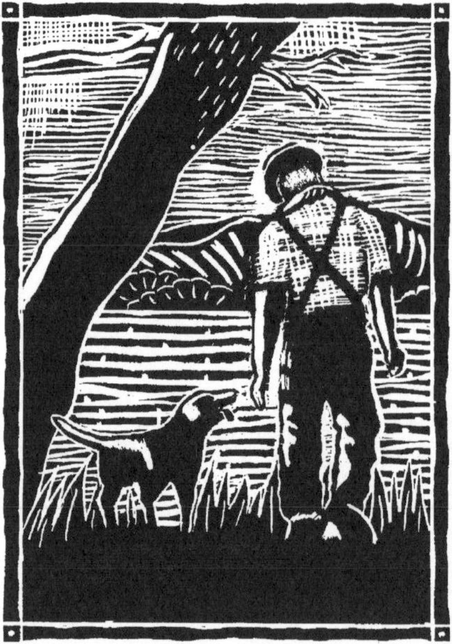

I've learned . . .

. . . to keep looking ahead. There are still so many good books to read, sunsets to see, friends to visit, and old dogs to take walks with. —Age 86

. . . that people can change, so give them the benefit of the doubt. —Age 14

$\mathcal{N}$ever let the odds keep you
from pursuing what you
know in your heart you were
meant to do.

∞

$\mathcal{B}$e happy with what you
have while working for what
you want.

Have courage for the
greatest sorrow of life and
patience for the small one,
and when you have
laboriously accomplished
your daily task, go to sleep
in peace. God is awake.

—Victor Hugo

Encourage anyone who is trying to improve mentally, physically, or spiritually.

❧

Things turn out best for people who make the best of the way things turn out.

—Anonymous

$\mathcal{B}$elieve in miracles
but don't depend on
them.

Hope is a periscope which enables us to see over our present problems to future possibilities.

∾

To be without some of the things you want is an indispensable part of happiness.

—Bertrand Russell

$\mathcal{L}$et your children know that regardless of what happens, you will always be there for them.

❧

$\mathcal{A}h$, but a man's reach should exceed his grasp,
Or what's a heaven for?

—Robert Browning

*I*n all things it is
better to hope than
to despair.

—Goethe